Young Blood: Murder in the Woods

By Scott Wachtler

Hope You Like It

For Serena

Dear Beau,

Your thoughtful, considerate and gracious manner is an endearing quality rarely encountered in this era. We're very proud of you and your individuality.

Love, Mom and Dad.

— From the Countryside High School 1989 yearbook

Introduction

The following true-crime story was written using personal interviews with those involved, court documents, police reports, media reports, medical records and legal depositions. Nothing has been fictionalized or altered to make the story more enticing. Like any piece of non-fiction, the accuracy of the information is only as good as the source materials. Every attempt was made to speak with the key players in this story; it is notated within the story when participants declined to be interviewed.

This story was written as impartially as possible, laying out all the available facts of the case. I leave it up to you, the reader, to draw your own conclusions as to the fate of those involved.

Chapter 1: A Murder

Spring in Central Florida is not unlike summer in Central Florida, except there's usually a week or two where the nights are cool enough to wear a sweater or a light jacket. On the night of April 10, 1989, it was in the mid-60s—pleasant for a spring Florida evening—many residents in the working class neighborhood of Oldsmar likely had their windows open to let in the sea breeze when they heard gunshots coming from the abandoned sewer facility near National Orange Avenue and Lafayette Boulevard.

Around 10:14 p.m., Sherry McCracken was sleeping when she was awakened by the sound of the first gunshot. She heard two more and then called the police. The Pinellas County Sheriff's Office logged her call and sent an officer out to the woods near the area of the sewer tanks.

The overgrown and wooded area was known by police and residents as a teen hangout. Drinking, pot smoking and probably more than one teenage love affair took place at this site, which looked out onto Safety Harbor. However, the officer who was dispatched to investigate found nothing suspicious and the call was cleared.

Had the responding officer done a better job, he or she would have found the bodies of 16-year-old William "Billy" Casey Jr. and his friend, 15-year-old Daniel Yockey.

A little more than an hour later, police received a 911 call concerning the same location. 17-year-old Beau Staples was calling from a pay phone at an Albertson's grocery store parking lot. He was there with his friend, 16-year-old Josh Walther. According to Beau, he and Josh, along with Billy Casey and Dan Yockey, had been out in the woods near the abandoned sewer plant earlier that night when they, too, heard the gunshots. All the boys ran and only Beau and Josh made it back to Beau's car. Beau told the police that as he and Josh fled the area in his father's 1979 white Chevy Impala Caprice Classic, someone in a pickup truck gave chase, but Beau managed to lose the truck when they pulled out into traffic. Once they felt they were safe, they called the police.

Beau told police that they didn't know what had happened to their friends, but he and Josh feared that they were in danger.

The officer on the phone advised Beau and Josh to stay where they were and they would send a police car out to the Albertson's to take their statement and then drive them to the site so police could search for their friends.

Other neighbors besides Sherry McCracken reported that they, too, heard shots coming from the sewer tank that night. Jack Milligan heard four loud shots around the same time his neighbor did. He walked outside and stood on the corner. He could make out a car parked at the dead end and he watched as it pulled out onto National Orange Avenue. He couldn't identify the make of the car, but he could tell it was a white or cream colored, older model General Motors vehicle. He said the car was not speeding and he could clearly see two people inside. As the car came to the intersection, the headlights came on and the driver turned right onto Lafayette Boulevard.

Gordon Metzker first heard two shots and then two more before he walked outside where he heard one more shot and saw a flash of fire near the wooded area. Soon after that, he watched two people get inside what he thought was a white Chevy Impala and drive away, making a right onto Lafayette Boulevard from National Orange Avenue.

Christopher Cloran heard a few shots and went outside where he heard a voice yell what he thought was "move out now!" He told police that he saw a white vehicle parked at the dead end and heard two people talking back and forth.

None of these other people who heard shots reported seeing a pick-up truck following the white Chevy Impala Caprice Classic, or that it appeared to be chased.

One of the officers who met up with Beau and Josh in the Albertson's parking lot was Deputy Robert Frist. He described both of the boys as nervous and excitable. One of them would start the story and the other would finish it. At times, Deputy Frist said it was difficult to determine who told him what, but the story was growing more elaborate since the initial 911 call.

Joining Deputy Frist was Patrol Sgt. Norman D. Romanosky, who spoke to Josh Walther before the police escorted the teens back to the location in the woods.

According to the story Beau and Josh told the police, all four of them went to the location because they heard a rumor there were marijuana plants growing near the sewer tanks. As they were searching, all four boys spread out. After a few minutes of searching Beau and Josh said they heard Billy Casey start yelling and shortly after that came the first gunshot. All four boys took off in different directions.

Beau and Josh breathlessly told the officers that they barely made it back to the car and then had to speed away once they saw the pickup truck following them. Beau told police that they knew they were being followed because when they sped up, the pickup truck sped up. They drove around the area of Belcher Road, which would have been somewhat busy around that time of night, until they lost sight of the truck that was chasing them. Neither Josh nor Beau could describe the make or model, or give a better description of the pickup truck.

Police working on the investigation determined that Billy Casey was wanted for escaping the Pinellas County Juvenile Detention Facility. Dan Yockey had no record but Josh provided the police with the address and phone number to Dan's apartment. They called hoping that he had made it home, but there was no answer.

Beau and Josh agreed to show the police the location in the woods so police could search for their friends. They first dropped Beau's car off at a nearby Kmart parking lot and then the teens got into the police cruiser to take the officers to the location. From the back of the police cruiser, Beau and Josh led police to the dead end road where a heavy wire cable barred entry to the sewer facility.

By this time, a helicopter hovered over the site, shining a light into the woods, and dozens of police officers, including two dogs from the k-9 unit, were searching the area for Billy Casey and Dan Yockey.

Beau and Josh were told to wait in the back of the police cruiser while the search was going on. The two teens could hear the police chatter coming in over the radio as the police searched for their friends. Within minutes, the police found something.

Chapter 2: A Setup

There was never any pot in the woods. It was a lie made up by Josh to get Billy out to the location. Since Billy had been on the run from the Pinellas County Juvenile Detention Facility and was always in need of money, Josh told him he could sell the pot to make some quick cash. Billy probably jumped at the chance, regardless of how far-fetched the idea might have sounded. Dan tagged along that night for the hell of it and for lack of anything better to do.

The day of the murder was a Monday, a school day, yet Josh spent most of it trying to track down Billy. Billy, of course, was not in school that day either. In fact, he hadn't been to school for nearly a month; ever since he had been on the run. Both his parents and the police questioned all of their son's friends but none of them said they knew where Billy was.

According to L. Roy Sullivan, a principal of one of the two high schools Billy attended before being locked up, "Billy was always in some kind of trouble and had problems with attendance and fighting."

Campus Police Officer David Krieger, who was stationed at Billy's first high school, described Billy as "a problem at the school," and had caught him drawing swastikas and anarchy symbols on the walls.

"He was not a nice kid," the same officer told the St. Petersburg Times days after the murder.

Billy had been placed in juvenile custody for a string of petty burglaries and for taking a golf cart on a joy ride and wrecking it. He allegedly escaped the juvenile detention facility through an opening in a ceiling light fixture while nobody was watching.

At first, the 16-year-old planned to get out of town and disappear, but he ended up staying local. The good-looking teen spent his time on the run juggling more than two girls who considered themselves his girlfriend—one of whom he said he planned to marry—and getting from place to place by bumming rides from anyone he could. Friends with a couch or a spare room provided a place to stay for short periods of time, but he mostly stayed with an older friend of his named David McLinch, who was known by police to be heavily involved with a local group who identified themselves as skinheads.

In fact, many of Billy's friends identified themselves as skinheads. In the late 1980s skinhead culture was hitting its peak. A year before the murder in the woods, talk-show host Geraldo Rivera got his nose broken during a fight that erupted on an episode of his show focusing on the skinhead phenomenon.

Twenty-five years later, one of Billy's best friends, Scott Calcaterra, remembers a very different Billy than the one portrayed by the authority figures in his life.

"He was probably one of the funniest guys you'd ever want to meet," he says. "He would do anything to brighten your day, even if it was at his expense. Even if he was going to get in trouble for it, he didn't care as long as you thought it was funny. I'm not saying he was stupid, he was just that kind of guy."

Billy and Scott shared a love of punk rock music and bonded with the few others at school who were also into the punk scene.

"He was my locker partner because we didn't like a lot of the other people at school," Scott says. "We bonded hard. He was my best friend."

While on the run, Billy's network of mostly older friends were keeping his whereabouts secret from Billy's family and the authorities, and made it easy for him to hang out during the day and go to parties at night where beer, pot and LSD were in ample supply. Billy saw no reason to leave town just yet.

"I had a feeling Billy was going to be fine [living on the run]," Scott says. "He was good at easily adapting to things. In some aspects, he was way more mature than a lot of us were at the time because of all he'd been though. With all the trouble he got into, this was almost like nothing to him."

Josh knew that Billy had been hiding out at friends' houses. It was only a matter of time before he found him for Beau.

Chris Conover knew Billy Casey, but had only met Josh the night before and wasn't sure why he was calling him looking for Billy.

"I asked him why he wanted to know," Conover recounted. "He was just like, 'Well, I really need to get ahold of him. It's important.' And he got angry, so I told him I'd call around."

Conover called about five numbers that Billy had left with him the day before. The person who answered the last number said Billy had just left.

According to Scott, the last time he saw Billy was only hours before Billy met up with Beau, Josh and Dan to look for the pot plants.

"He told me he was going out to meet with some friends and I figured Beau was involved because he knew I didn't like the guy and knew not to talk to me about him," Scott says. "Billy would tell me that he and Beau did this, and he and Beau did that, and I would tell him, 'I don't want to hear anything about this asshole.' So after a while he just stopped mentioning what he and Beau were doing."

In the days before the ubiquity of cell phones, or even pagers, it wasn't always easy to find someone who didn't want to be found. Josh's search for Billy eventually led him to the condo complex where single mother Carey Yockey rented an apartment with her two sons, Gary and Dan. Josh knew Gary from school and asked him if Billy had been by. Gary told Josh that Billy and Dan had been hanging out all day but they were now out. Josh knew that he had Billy's location. He asked Gary to tell Billy he was looking for him and to call him when they returned.

Josh's next call was to Beau, who was working his after-school job at the Kmart in Oldsmar. They agreed that once Josh heard back from Billy, he would tell him about the pot plants in the woods and then, once Beau was off work, they would meet up at the Yockey apartment.

Beau was the only one of the teens with a driver's license and access to a car. After he got off work, around 9:30 p.m., he picked Josh up at his house and the two went to Oshman's Sporting Goods store in the Countryside Mall, where Beau purchased a box of five shotgun shells. He loaded the shotgun in the parking lot and threw away the box in a ditch by the road.

Since neither one of them knew where the Yockeys lived, they went to a payphone and found three listings for Yockey in the phonebook. They went to the closest of the three addresses and found Billy and Dan sitting on a wall outside, playing with a neighbor's dog.

With nothing else planned for the night, going out into the woods looking for pot plants likely seemed an interesting adventure to Billy, who was ready to go, and unaware that the two people he considered friends had been planning to murder him for over a week.

"Before we got in the car, Billy asked if it was okay if Dan tagged along, and Josh immediately said 'yeah, sure,'" Beau recalls decades later.

Beau remembers asking Billy, 'what's up with this dude?' "Billy told me 'it's all right. He's straight,'" Beau recounts.

With Billy and Dan now in the back seat, Beau looked over the top of the car at Josh, who was about to get into the passenger seat. Beau put his hands up as if to ask, "What now?"

"I forgot exactly what I said, but I basically said, 'This is over, this isn't going to work and this isn't going to happen.'"

However, according to Beau, Josh was still ready to go through with their plan. Beau described Josh's reaction as "scrunching up his face, smiling" and making a pirate-like throat slash by running his thumb horizontally across his neck; a gesture that Beau took to mean that their plan was likely still on and that Josh would be the one to take care of Dan.

At around 200 pounds and about 6 feet tall, Josh was a big 16-year-old who lifted weights every other day. He was also into punk rock music and had been known at nearby East Lake High School as Big Josh, the kid who sometimes wore a mohawk hairdo and Doc Martin combat boots.

Since Josh was the only one who was familiar with the sewer plant, he gave Beau directions. Meanwhile, Beau's mind was racing. Was the murder on? Was it off? Dan wasn't supposed to be there and was never part of the plan.

"That poor fucker was in the wrong place at the wrong time," Beau now says.

Beau says that although he and Billy had had "words" a few times earlier that week, Billy didn't seem to suspect anything during the drive to the sewer plant, but he knew that Billy sometimes carried a knife and a gun that he found during one of the robberies that eventually sent him to the Pinellas Regional Juvenile Detention Center.

"On the way there I asked them if anyone was carrying any guns or knives because I'm thinking about killing this guy and maybe he's thinking about killing me," Beau says. "I was starting to get hyper paranoid."

Billy said he wasn't carrying anything and likely wasn't surprised by the question because he was aware that Beau knew his history. As Beau parked the car, Billy went for Beau's camouflage hoodie jacket, but he stopped him.

"No, I'm going to wear that," he said looking at Billy through the rear view mirror. "I'm wearing a white T-shirt and I need something to make me less noticeable out there."

While Beau and Josh had a conversation near the car, Dan and Billy waited at the heavy wire cable that served to block the entrance to the abandoned sewer facility. Dan was unable to hear what Beau and Josh were talking about.

"This could be a setup," Billy told Dan, probably starting to feel a little suspicious.

Dan didn't know what kind of setup it could be. At this point, he was unaware that Billy and Beau had argued about Billy flirting with Beau's ex-girlfriend. As far as he knew, Beau and Billy had been tight. In fact, earlier that day, Billy told Dan that Beau was one of the friends who helped get him things like cigarettes and snuff while he was on the run from the police.

"What do you mean?" Dan asked about the possibility of a setup.

"I'll tell you about it later," Billy said.

Josh, now wearing a camouflage bandana, met up with Billy and Dan at the cable and all three easily ducked under it and entered the woods. Beau stayed behind in order to turn the car around so they wouldn't have to back it out on the narrow dead end when they left.

The woods were dark and the area was not well lit. According to Josh's lie, the pot plants were near the abandoned sewer plant and the water tank near a heavily-graffitied concrete building.

It didn't take long before Dan began to get very skeptical about the story, and admitted that the idea did occur to him that they were out in the middle of the woods, in the dark of night, looking for marijuana, and nobody had thought to bring a flashlight.

Beau met up with the trio a little later. By now he was wearing the camouflage hoodie and carrying a loaded olive-drab 12-gauge Mossberg 500 shotgun slung over his shoulder with a military style M-1 sling.

Chapter 3: A Friendship/A Rivalry

Beau and Billy met a few years earlier while they were working at Burger King. Beau had not yet met Josh, but Billy and Josh also knew each other. It was Beau who Billy called for a ride once he escaped the detention center, and it was Beau who first found Billy a place to stay while on the run. Beau lied to the police, to his own parents and to Billy's parents when they questioned him about where Billy might be hiding out.

"During the next couple of weeks [after the escape] the police would pull me over, looking for Billy," Beau said. "They even knocked on my parents' door at 2 a.m. looking for him."

Beau describes himself and Billy as being close friends before Billy was put into the detention center. They shared a love of the military and a love of guns. They would hang out in the woods and "play army" or camp.

"Beau was interested in all kinds of different people and all different social interactions," Beau's mother, Johnnie Sue Staples says. "I had met the boy [Billy] one time when [Beau] brought him to the house and introduced him to us. That was the only time. After we found out a little more about him, my husband told Beau to not have anything else to do with him because he wasn't the sort of person we wanted him to be friends with."

Billy's troubled family life and involvement with skinheads were the warning signs Beau's parents warned him against, however, Beau and Billy's friendship continued without his parents' knowledge.

"I'm not trying to blame the victim, but [Billy's family] came from a different kind of background than we did—emotionally, socially and every which way," Johnnie Sue says. "That was probably fascinating to Beau, and it wasn't the best situation, of course, and it certainly didn't turn out that way. I think he got into a situation with Billy that he didn't know how to get out of and withdraw from."

Beau recalled that he and Billy bonded early on and that they each considered the other good friends. They both had the same digital watch and that they each used to set their alarms to 10:20 p.m. every night.

"I don't remember what the meaning behind why we did that was," Beau now admits. "It might have been the time a girl we knew got off work or something like that; it was just something kids used to do, but every night at 10:20 my alarm would go off and I would think about Billy's alarm going off too."

To Beau, ratting on his friend to the police or their parents was out of the question. That would have gone against his teenage notion of honor and duty towards your friends, whom he saw as his army buddies—an ideal likely learned from the hours of war and gangster movies Beau says he used to watch. In his room hung posters of George C. Scott as General Patton and John Wayne from *The Green Berets*, along with a poster from the movie *Scarface*, three movies he admits to watching hundreds of times.

Unlike Billy, Beau was a popular kid who somehow managed to float between all the sharply territorial cliques at the lofty, affluent Countryside High School, where it was very common to see BMWs, Mercedes and Cameros in the student parking lot. In this very socially segregated high school, Beau was an enigma who was equally liked by the jocks, media nerds, freaks, geeks, punks, R.O.T.C cadets and even teachers. He was an honor student who seemed to be a very mature and responsible teen; the kind of teen mothers like to know their sons were friends with, or their daughters were dating.

"We had kind of hoped that some of Beau would rub off on Billy," Billy's step-mother, Sherry Casey says.

Even today his slow and thoughtful way of speaking retains a subtle southern charm and an air of southern hospitality.

Beau's mother describes her son as "a southern gentleman."

"He was as good as any child you'd want to be," Johnnie Sue Staples says of her son. "It was very seldom that I even had to discipline or reprimand him. He was so good. As a teenager he never left the house without telling me he loved me. He was just a good child."

Students at Countryside High School looked up to him and liked him too because he was funny as the co-anchor of the school's weekly morning news show. As an anchor he adopted a smarmy and dry Chevy Chase-like persona that could be funny and also a little cruel in the era before school bullying became outlawed. As a member of the R.O.T.C, he had hopes of becoming a U.S. Marine Corps Intelligence officer and possibly going on to a career in the C.I.A.

To many, Beau was known as "the army guy" who was deeply involved in all things having to do with the military.

"It's almost hard to believe in this post-Columbine world, but I remember Beau brought an unloaded bazooka into school for R.O.T.C show-and-tell," recalls Carl Zimmermann, the Media Studies teacher, and now Florida State Representative, who worked closely with Beau and all the students on the morning show. "Unless he was in his R.O.T.C uniform he was always dressed in a button-down shirt and sometimes a tie and he mostly wore slacks, not jeans."

"In R.O.T.C. there was a sense the instructors gave us that when you're out there and you're wearing this uniform on Tuesdays, people aren't just judging you, they're judging the entire program," Beau recalls. "It was that way in my senior year in Mr. Zimmermann's class…it was like it wasn't just me if I did something stupid, it would reflect back to the program."

However, not every clique welcomed Beau into their fold. Many of Billy's skinhead friends came from nearby East Lake High School. Scott Calcaterra still remembers taking an immediate disliking towards Beau and his attempts at ingratiating himself into their group.

"Cookie-cutter, clean-cut kid, right? He seem[ed] that way," Scott says. "At first, that was one of the reasons I didn't like him. He was from a totally different background than all of us, and when you're that age, you don't want to hang around with people from such a different background as you."

The first time Scott met Beau he was with Billy, and Beau was videotaping or taking pictures of the group.

"I told him to stop it and he kept doing it," Scott says. "I almost fought him the first time I met him. Me and Billy and our group of friends, we were good kids back then, but we were also trouble makers. Some of our friends were pretty hardened criminals and considered themselves white power skinheads. A lot of us had F.B.I. files, and here was this guy we didn't know sitting there with a video camera taking video or taking pictures of us. That was just wrong. So no, I didn't like him, and then I just got a really bad vibe about him. When I found out Billy was murdered, the first person who popped into my head was Beau Staples. I just didn't like him from the start... He was always talking about guns and becoming a Marine."

At the start of his senior year Beau had a lot going for him. He was dating a pretty girl, Mary Zigmond, with whom he was planning to go to the prom. He had already purchased tickets for them to attend Grad Night, a now-defunct Disney World event where Florida high school seniors got to enjoy the park until the early morning hours. However, after the winter break, cracks started to show in Beau and Mary's relationship. Zimmerman remembers the change as "almost overnight."

"After Columbine, teachers were trained to look for warning signs that kids might be in distress," Zimmerman said. "But back then, you just didn't get involved."

The problems with Mary came to a head before the winter break.

"He was starting to get possessive and wanted more of a commitment from me," Zigmond said later in her statement to police. "We fought a lot… We saw each other off and on, but eventually I broke it off."

It was around the time Beau's relationship with Mary was beginning to crumble that Billy escaped from detention. Mary and Billy had known each other since grade school and it was Billy who Mary sought out to talk to about her problems with Beau. At a party they all attended, Mary got drunk and Beau was furious and refused to drive her home. At one point, Mary and Billy went to a bedroom where they talked about her problems with Beau.

It didn't take long before high school rumors began to crop up and word got around that Mary and Billy had been doing more than talking.

"Mary was a really sweet girl," Zimmermann says. "But she wasn't perceived that way by other people...somehow people thought she was loose. Everybody was so surprised that Beau was going out with Mary."

Once the rumors began to circulate, Billy snuck up to Mary's window at 2 a.m. to tell her that Beau was aware of the rumors and was pissed off. The next morning, Beau drove Mary to school and the two fought, even though Mary insisted nothing sexual happened between her and Billy. The two went their separate ways once they got to school and didn't talk for the rest of the day.

After school, Mary met up with Billy at one of the apartments where he was hiding out and he told her that Beau was getting angrier about the party and the rumor that they had slept together.

"He told me that I shouldn't have to deal with the way Beau was treating me," Mary said.

"I felt like he was sleeping with my girl and he was trying to drive a wedge between us," Beau says, explaining his anger. "And they were both laughing at me behind my back and lying to me."

Within the next few days, Beau and Mary saw each other off and on, and each time they fought. Eventually Mary told Beau that she wanted to break up, but that didn't stop Beau from calling her at her parents' house or staring at her menacingly during lunch period.

Mary's older brother, Chris, also got involved. "Beau was being a real jerk at school," he told investigators. "I told him: 'leave my sister alone. Don't talk to her, look at her—just leave her alone!'"

But Beau didn't let it go. On a Sunday morning, he called Mary to confront her, again, about the rumor and also to tell her that Billy was going around telling people she was a whore and bragging that they had slept together.

"I knew Billy wouldn't have cut me down like that because we had known each other a long time and had been good friends," she later told police.

On the phone with her irate ex-boyfriend, she admitted that Billy did kiss her the night of the party, but they did not have sex. During the ensuing argument, Mary hung up on Beau.

He called back and they argued some more.

"You're fucking going to pay for this," were the last words Mary was to hear from Beau Staples.

Chapter 4: A Plan

Beau decided about a week before the murder that Billy deserved to die for "fooling around" with his girlfriend.

"He couldn't be trusted anymore. He was getting reckless," he told prosecutors at his deposition almost a year after the murder. "[Billy] had escaped from the JDC. And he was just going around causing trouble, just, I don't know, just being a tough guy, trying to be a tough guy…trying to throw his weight around…he would make passes at my girlfriend. He was getting to where he just couldn't be trusted anymore. Our friendship had always been where we could trust each other, trust each other with our lives pretty much. We were all really close, and he just deviated from that."

While Beau admitted to prosecutors that he didn't consider Josh a best friend, he did confide in him about the problems he was having with Billy because Josh and Billy also knew each other.

"Josh didn't kill Billy, I did, but I wouldn't have killed Billy without Josh's constant encouragement," Beau says.

Beau alleges that he and Josh first thought up the plan to kill Billy while they were sitting behind a 7-

Eleven convenience store on the Friday before the murder. Josh, who went to trial on the case in 1992, denies ever having been in on any plan to kill Billy.

According to Beau, it was Josh who came up with the first plan. They were going to take Billy to the Tampa International Airport parking garage, knock him unconscious and throw him off the roof. However, later that day, Beau gained access to the Mossberg 500 shotgun.

The true ownership of the gun was a question that at first confused police, but through interviews and court documents, it's shown that the owner of the shotgun was Billy Peak, who lent it to a friend of Billy Casey's and Beau's named Jeffery Faust. Faust lent the shotgun to Casey and he wanted it back when he discovered that the police were looking for Billy. He told Beau to get the shotgun back from Billy if he saw him around. At that time, Billy was staying with yet another friend, and Beau and Josh went there to pick up the shotgun.

When they got there, Beau saw Billy and decided to give him one more chance to be honest about what had happened between him and Mary.

"I also wanted to see if he had any plans to leave town because if he did, I wouldn't have to do anything. I thought that he and Mary were seeing each other—that's what I thought the truth was," Beau says. "[After we talked] and I realized he wasn't leaving, I still thought the whole truth wasn't being told to me."

With the shotgun now in his trunk, wrapped in a towel, Beau decided to scrap the Tampa International Airport plan.

"We had gotten the gun, and it seemed a lot easier now," Beau said on the stand at Josh's trial. "I was going to use the shotgun to shoot Billy Casey."

The fact that Beau returned carrying a shotgun didn't seem to faze Billy or Dan. Billy likely recognized the shotgun as being the one Jeffery Faust had lent him, and Beau was supposed to return it. Dan was no stranger to weapons, either. His brother kept a shotgun and ammunition in the apartment and he figured Beau brought the gun to protect the group while they were out searching for the marijuana.

"Nobody said anything about the shotgun," Beau says. "I mean, it was pretty much common anyway, guns with us, it's just that we all had guns."

While Beau was looking for the others he released the safety on the shotgun and chambered the first round. He entered the area from a different direction than the other three had, which investigators would later wrongly conclude was because Beau might have hidden the shotgun somewhere in the area prior, or that he came to the area from a different direction in order to ambush the others.

"I had never been out there before in my life," Beau later said. "By the time I turned the car around they were out of sight and I just followed the dirt path out there. It took me ten or fifteen minutes to find them because I got lost."

Josh was on top of one of the concrete buildings pretending to get an overview of the area to try to see where the pot may be, while Dan and Billy were futilely looking around.

"This sucks," Billy said. "Let's go!"

Dan agreed. He had had enough of the useless search. "This is a wild goose chase. Let's just leave," he said.

"Let's just have another look," Josh said, stalling for time.

Beau played along with the ruse of looking for pot by swinging the shotgun through the bushes as if he were searching for the plants.

Eventually they all agreed to leave. Josh led the way out and walked to the right on the path. Billy was a little further back and to the left. Beau was behind the two in the center, while Dan was bringing up the rear.

As a member of the R.O.T.C and someone who had hoped to go into the Marines, this was hardly the first time Beau had fired a shotgun. But it was the first time he used one to kill someone.

With Billy only feet in front of him, Beau brought the shotgun up and noticed Josh looking back at him. Realizing what was about to happen, Josh covered his ears and quickly side-stepped off the trail. Beau said he first aimed the shotgun towards Billy's head, but then lowered it at Billy's back and pulled the trigger. Beau remembers pulling the trigger, but can't remember hearing the blast.

"I remember smoke and then lowering the shotgun and then not seeing Billy standing there anymore…he just dropped, just like dead weight," Beau recalls. "I could hear Billy yelling…and he's in pain."

He didn't think it would be this messy, nor that the first shot would fail to kill Billy immediately. The plan was that Beau would shoot Billy with one shot and he would die, just like people did in the movies he'd watched so many times.

"We didn't want him to know what hit him," Beau says. "The desensitization to violence made it easy to pull the trigger without thinking too much. Actually seeing someone get shot is something else entirely. I never thought more than one shot would be needed."

Billy was now lying on the ground, face down, yelling. According to the autopsy, the blast from the shotgun hit Billy in the right side of his back and went through his chest, piercing the lower part of his lung. Dr. Joan Wood, who performed the autopsy, said that the first shot didn't kill Billy Casey immediately, but it would have eventually—within minutes.

Beau racked the shotgun again, trotted up to his dying former friend and, at very close range, shot him a second time in the back. Billy was no longer yelling. Instinctively, Beau racked the shotgun again, ejecting the second used cartridge.

Dr. Wood determined the second shot was a sharp upward wound that struck Billy in the upper left side of his back and fractured multiple ribs on the right side of his body. Portions of the wadding from the shotgun shell severed the brain stem into two, high into the neck. The shot would have caused instant paralysis and would have made it impossible for Billy to scream or breathe. Death would have come to Billy Casey seconds after the second gunshot.

With Billy now silenced, the gravity of what he had just done was starting to hit Beau, and along with that reality, a new sound came into focus. He could hear Dan Yockey behind him, hyperventilating and repeating, "Oh my God. Oh my God. Oh my God. Oh my God!"

"I turn around and I look at him and I go 'oh, man, now what?'"

Chapter 5: An Alarm

Dan Yockey saw it all clearly, and it all happened very quickly. He was only a few feet away from Beau when he saw him raise the shotgun, point it in Billy's direction and fire. He saw Billy go down and heard Billy's screams. He watched as Beau shuffled up to Billy's body lying face-down in the dirt and fire the second shot into Billy's back to stop him from screaming. Dan assumed he was next.

He ran.

"I was running, zigzagging and running for my life," Dan said.

Dan ran towards the heavily spray-painted building and the water tank, but he ended up running directly into a fence that was covered with vegetation. Beau caught up with him and pointed the shotgun in his face.

"Don't shoot me, please don't shoot me!" Dan pleaded.

Beau was holding Dan against the fence with one hand and the shotgun with the other.

"It's not loaded," Beau lied to try to calm Dan down and tell him what he wanted to hear, but Dan didn't believe him. Beau lowered the shotgun to his hip, pulled Dan off the fence and brought him out into the open where Dan assumed he was going to be shot for being a witness to Billy's murder.

"I wasn't going to shoot Dan Yockey," Beau says. "I just—I had had enough of that, I mean I wasn't going to kill two people out there that night…I didn't even know the guy. I wasn't going to kill him. I figured…Dan was Josh's responsibility, because he said it was okay that he could come along. I wasn't going to kill Dan."

That's when Josh came running towards Dan. Dan tried to run away, but Josh was faster and stronger. He tackled Dan, pinned him to the ground and began punching him in the face. Dan tried to kick Josh off, but he couldn't. He managed to kick Josh on the side of his head. In the struggle, Josh lost the camouflage bandana he was wearing, but he was overpowering Dan. He was now sitting on top of Dan with his hands around Dan's neck, strangling him. Dan was beginning to run out of fight.

"It is incredible to see somebody fighting for his life. It is the most horrific thing to see," Beau says. "I mean [Dan] was fighting back with everything he had, but he just couldn't win because he was a smaller guy, and Josh was pretty big."

By this time, Beau was in shock. He remembers not getting a very clear look at what Josh was doing to Dan because they were scuffling in high grass. Plus, by now Beau was busy throwing up. Beau testified that he did see Josh kicking Dan, but Josh denied that at the trial. However, Beau remembers Josh calling out to him.

"Beau, come here and help me," Beau alleges Josh called.

By the time Beau made his way over to Josh, Dan wasn't moving. Beau raised the shotgun and punched Dan in the stomach with it, but unlike his R.O.T.C training had likely taught him, Beau had not put the safety on and he still had his finger on the trigger. As he hit Dan, the shotgun went off a third time. The blast was so close to Beau's head he almost killed himself. But he was just momentarily deafened and blinded.

"I was sick and now I was numb," Beau said. "Josh asked me 'did you shoot him, did you shoot him?' and I said 'No. No, this is over. Let's get out of here."

Beau assumed Josh had strangled Dan to death and they were leaving two dead bodies in the woods. At Josh's trial, his defense attorney argued that Josh feared for his life and the life of Dan's and he was only trying to silence Dan so Beau wouldn't shoot them both.

Josh took off towards the car and Beau followed, still carrying the shotgun. The empty shell rattled inside the gun next to the remaining two shells. Out of instinct, he racked the gun and chambered the next round, discharging the third cartridge close to the other two near Billy Casey's body. This time, he put the safety on.

Beau was having trouble keeping up with Josh, who was faster. Beau was also slowed down by constantly throwing up and once he was done being sick, he managed to get stuck in the mud up to his ankles, ruining his sneakers.

When he caught up to Josh, who was already at the car, he handed him the keys and the shotgun, telling him to put the gun in the trunk. As he was taking off his muddy shoes—concerned that he would get his father's car dirty—the alarm on Beau's digital watch went off.

It was 10:20 p.m.

The alarm that he and Billy had agreed to set was ringing and bringing into focus everything that Beau Staples had just done.

"It went off and I stopped. I stopped and said, 'Holy *shit*! What'd I do? What the *hell* did I do? That's when it all hit me…I thought 'Wow, I'm in trouble. This is bigger than me.' It feels like there's just a dump truck of mud being dropped on you. It was smothering at that point."

The two got into the car and slowly made their way out of the area. Beau remembers seeing someone standing in front of the house on the corner, likely Jack Milligan, watching them leave.

Josh later testified that when he got in the car, he was in shock and unable to speak, yet Beau was talking a lot.

"He was saying that he didn't mean to do that. That it was a stupid thing to do, and that I had to help him," Josh testified.

Beau doesn't believe Josh was in shock because he remembers Josh having a "stupid grin on his face like he was amused."

Beau admits to taking charge in concocting the story they would later tell the cops. As they were driving, he used Josh as a sounding board to see whether the story sounded believable. But before they could call the police they needed to return the shotgun to the person who originally lent it to Billy, Jeffery Faust.

Faust took one look at Beau and Josh and knew something wasn't right. Not only did they both look like hell, but Beau was also missing his shoes.

"When [Beau] was handing me the shotgun he became real nervous and edgy and looked really abnormal, so I told him I didn't want the shotgun," Faust testified at Josh's trial.

Now they needed to get rid of the murder weapon. Beau drove to the Courtney Campbell Causeway and Josh threw the weapon off the bridge.

On the drive back over the causeway to Clearwater, Beau went over the story they would tell the police, and he was beginning to regain his composure. He admits that Josh didn't help much with the "ridiculous" story.

"Josh wasn't a particularly creative person, so he was not really helpful in making up the story," Beau said. "I wasn't nearly as scared as I should have been and I think that's a product of not fully comprehending the gravity of what we had done, or the consequences. I wasn't even thinking of prison."

On the phone with 911, Beau made sure to sound scared. Josh was standing close enough to hear what

Beau was telling the operator. The call lasted about three minutes and afterwards they calmly sat on the curb and waited for the police to arrive.

They both seemed to relax a bit, even taking time to hit on a pretty woman on her way into the grocery store.

"I said to her, 'What's up?' and she looked at me and kept walking. Me and Josh both looked at her back as she walked away and said 'Bitch' at the same time, and then looked at each other and chuckled," Beau said. "We were still teenage boys."

Before the police arrived, they rehearsed the story.

"I made Josh repeat it," Beau says. "I asked him, 'are you cool with that?' and he said, 'Fuck, yeah.'"

In spite of their inexperience and the unforeseen setbacks, their story had a good chance of holding up.

However, what they didn't know at the time was that Dan Yockey was not dead.

Chapter 6: A Witness

In the hour before Beau placed the call to the police, Dan had regained consciousness. At first he was unsure whether Beau and Josh were still in the woods looking to kill him, but he eventually found his way out to a main road where, dazed and very confused, he tried to find a ride home.

From the chatter coming over the radio, it was becoming obvious to Beau and Josh that the police had found Billy's body but that Dan was not in the woods.

"When I realized that Yockey wasn't dead I was relieved but scared," Beau writes in a recent letter. "I told Josh, 'We're fucked.' And I wondered what was going to happen."

Earlier that night, before Josh and Beau tracked Billy down to the Yockey apartment, Beau says Josh gave him a "lucky" arrowhead. Once they became suspects, about six deputies approached the patrol car and asked the two teens to step out. They frisked both of them and found Beau's lucky arrowhead.

"Did you find this out here?" one of the deputies asked Beau.

The smug 17-year-old who wasn't a huge fan of law enforcement answered "Naw, that's my lucky arrowhead."

The deputy raised an eyebrow and incredulously asked, "Really?"

"I guess not so lucky…" was Beau's response.

The two were handcuffed and moved to the back of a different patrol car where the radio was turned down. They would soon be transported to the Sheriff's Administration Building for further questioning.

"That's when I knew they considered us suspects and we were in a lot of trouble," Beau said.

Sgt. Romanosky found the body of Billy Casey, along with the three spent shotgun shells. Also found at the scene were Josh's camouflage bandana and a pack of Camel cigarettes, later found to belong to Dan.

Also found at the scene was the top of a red plastic pitchfork; the type used as an accessory to a devil Halloween costume. This item, probably left over from previous teen activities at the site led many to erroneously speculate that Billy's murder had satanic undertones—a rumor that spread throughout the two schools Beau and Josh attended.

Having already gotten Dan's address from Josh, Deputy Frist requested that police be sent to the address to see if Dan had made it home, or if someone from his family had heard from him.

Dan had made it home. He told his brother, Gary, what had happened and was still in shock.

"I just really wanted to sleep," he said.

When deputies arrived at the apartment, they found Gary watching over Dan, who was asleep on the couch. The deputies noticed that Gary was guarding Dan with a shotgun and a butterfly knife, in fear that Beau or Josh would come looking for him.

Gary said his brother had come home "around 12:30 in the morning" and looked "pretty beat up. One of his eyes was red. His ear bruised. He had scratches on his neck. He was dirty and his voice was hoarse," Gary told police.

As police were getting ready to take Dan to the station for questioning, Carry Yockey came home and saw her son being put into the back of a police car.

"What happened?" she asked Dan.

"Bill is dead!" A scared Dan told his mother.

On the way to the station, Dan told the officers what he had seen in the woods at the abandoned sewer facility.

Back at the scene, Detective Wayne Desmarais arrived and took the lead on the case. Frist showed him Billy's body, where fire ants were beginning to cover Billy's wounds, and filled him in on the story Beau and Josh had told them. He also told Desmarais that deputies were on the way to the Yockey apartment to find the other witness.

Desmarais wanted to take a look at Beau's car at the Kmart parking lot, to see if there were any clues there. On his way, he was radioed that Dan had been found and police were taking him to the station for questioning.

At the station, Dan told Desmarais everything that had happened, and how he awoke alone and paralyzed with fear that Beau and Josh were still out in the woods waiting to kill him. He had never been out to the area before and had no idea where he was. He found his way to a main road and saw people working late at a Pizza Hut. He knocked on the door for help, but was told that they couldn't let him in after hours. He eventually made it to an Amoco gas station, about a mile away from the murder scene, where a customer took pity on him and offered to give him a ride home.

"He was a mess. He looked like he was all beat up," Ross McGaee said.

Lisa Parker, who worked the late shift at the station, described Dan's hair as being "all messed up."

"He looked as if he had been fighting," she said. "He was…a little muddy, really shaky and distressed."

During questioning, Desmarais noticed that Dan's voice was raspy, his right eye was bloodshot and that he had marks on his neck. Despite these injuries, Dan refused medical attention. When Dr. Wood, who was now doing her preliminary examination on Billy's body, heard this, she insisted that Dan be sent to the medical examiner's office to be looked at, so she could make sure he didn't have any dangerous swelling in his neck and she could determine whether his eyes contained the telltale marks that would indicate he had been choked unconscious.

By this time Beau and Josh were already at the station. The two were taken to a large office where the homicide detectives sat. Beau winked at Josh as they were led away. Beau remembers that Josh smiled back.

Before Beau or Josh were able to speak to their parents, they were both fingerprinted and dirt was taken from underneath their fingernails for analysis. Swabs were taken of their hands to check for gunshot residue. Beau's attorney later motioned to throw out this evidence since he was a minor at the time. That request eventually became moot.

When Beau did eventually call his mother, it was already late at night.

"He called me that night and said that he was going to be late, and that something had happened, and that he had to stay and talk to the police," Johnnie Sue says. "He said 'don't worry' and I said 'okay, I won't', but then I did worry. I was hearing helicopters and my husband and I didn't go back to sleep. Then I got the call the next morning, you know? They'd been questioning him all night. Without us there."

While they were being processed, Beau was still curious about whether they had found Dan yet and what, if anything, he had been telling them.

"Detective, let me ask you something. How many murders were there tonight?" Beau asked Corporal Bruce Hauck, who was assigned to watch over the suspects while at the station. It's likely that by this time Cpl. Hauck knew the answer to the question, but he played dumb and told Beau he didn't know what he was talking about.

"You should know," Cpl. Hauck responded. "Because you were there."

Beau did not respond. He admits that he was becoming more and more scared as the investigators were trying to get him to talk about what had happened.

"They don't read you your rights like in a T.V. show, they tell them to you in a conversation," he said. "[The detective] put his arm around me and was trying to be nice, and said 'now you understand, Beau, that an attorney could be appointed for you? Would you like something to drink, by the way?' But I didn't want to talk. I told him I wanted to wait for my parents and an attorney."

When he said he didn't want to talk, the detective became angry and slammed his hand down in front of Beau, scaring him even more, telling him that he was making a mistake by being difficult.

"They're good. They're so crafty. He really scared the hell out of me. I didn't know what was going to happen," Beau recalls.

Before Beau's parents arrived, Desmarais charged Beau with first degree murder and Josh with first degree murder and first degree attempted murder of Dan Yockey. However, Josh's first degree murder charge wouldn't stick because the judge felt there was not enough evidence to show that he had helped plan Billy's murder. Josh was eventually released on bail to await trial. In spite of their age, both would be tried as adults.

Beau's parents arrived at the station with Beau's brother Jeff. An officer escorted them into the room where Beau was being kept, and waited just outside the door. During the meeting the officer noted that he could hear and see Beau's father, Howard, asking his son a question.

"Did you shoot anybody last night?" Howard Staples asked his son.

The officer who overheard this conversation wrote in his report that Beau did not respond verbally, but shook his head in an up and down motion, answering in the affirmative.

Beau's mother says she doesn't remember this and Beau says it didn't happen this way. Later, Beau's attorney motioned for this to be thrown out and the motion was granted on the grounds that Beau should have been allowed a private meeting with his parents.

Within days of being arrested, Beau was transferred from the juvenile detention center to the maximum security wing of the Pinellas County Jail with the regular prison population.

Chapter 7: A Prisoner

Beau Staples is now 42 years old. He has been behind bars longer than he's lived on the outside. He was allowed to graduate with the Countryside High School class of 1989—the first Pinellas County Jail prisoner in memory to ever get an actual high school diploma while in jail instead of a G.E.D—but he regrets never having gone to college.

"I feel like I'm smart enough, but I haven't had the opportunity in here," he says. "Correspondence courses are expensive and I don't want to ask my family for help. I've put them through enough."

Beau is mentioned three times in his yearbook. His senior picture shows a dimpled teen smiling confidently, while the group shot of his R.O.T.C class shows the flat-topped, almost 6-foot Beau standing tall in the back row with a pressed-lipped smile. His ears stick out a little, making him look even more boyish than he does in his senior picture.

Beau is not mentioned as the anchor of the morning news program, but the editors of the yearbook did include a senior message to Beau from his parents, sent prior to the murder.

Your thoughtful, considerate and gracious manner is an endearing quality rarely encountered in this era. We're very proud of you and your individuality.

Love, Mom and Dad

I was a year ahead of Beau in high school and in my first year of college when the story broke that he was involved in the murder of Billy Casey. Like many people, I assumed there was a misunderstanding, or an accident, because there was no way that someone as popular and as personable as Beau could have killed someone. However, as more of the story came out, hindsight began to come into focus and memories of Beau's fascination with guns, the military, and his veneer of being very righteous and principled began to make many, including me, think twice about his innocence.

For the last 15 years Beau has been one of 1,800 prisoners incarcerated at the Avon Park Correctional Institution in Avon Park, Florida. According to the warden, Beau and a roommate share an 8' x 5' cell. They each have a footlocker for their belongings and they share a bunk bed, a sink and a toilet. The prison is not air conditioned and there is one T.V. room on each floor. Except for the food, Beau said this prison is the nicest he's been to while in custody.

"We used to get good regular food and meat like pork chops occasionally, and things like that, but there were cutbacks a few years ago," he said. "Now the only meat we get is nutria and I won't eat that. It's nasty. I eat in the canteen. Where the food is a little better."

Nutria are rodents, also known as river rats. They are hunted for their pelts and their meat. They are considered an invasive species that are hunted in Louisiana in order to control their population. Their meat is lean and low in cholesterol, but, unsurprisingly, attempts to sell nutria meat to the public have been unsuccessful.

Despite the fact that Beau says Avon Park Correctional Institution is one of the nicer prisons he's experienced, to an outsider it still looks very much like a prison. The maximum security facility where Beau is located is encased in a double layer of chain link fence, topped by tight circles of razor wire. Inside the gates are concrete paths to the various buildings. Prisoners are only allowed to walk in the lanes painted on the side of the concrete path. Only prison staff is allowed to walk in the center.

The warden of the prison brought me to the building where Beau and I would talk. Beau was sitting on a bench with other prisoners in another section behind a chain link fence. Someone called his name and he came forward as the gate was opened. I noticed that he made sure to walk on the outside lane of the concrete path.

At first I didn't know how to acknowledge him. Do you exchange the same niceties with a convicted murderer who has spent almost 25 years in prison as you do with anyone you haven't seen in a long time? Would "Hey how's it going, good to see you!" still work? We shook hands and I mumbled a "good to see you" as we were led to an office where we talked for three and half hours about everything that led up to the murder and afterwards. We reminisced about old friends and teachers and talked about what the future may hold.

After more than a quarter of a century, Beau is much the way I remember him from high school. He still has the ability to make you like him, in spite of the fact that he is a convicted—and admitted—murderer.

Gone is the military-style flat-top I remembered. He's tall and thin. He keeps in shape with regular workouts and by being the captain of the prison softball team, which allows him time outdoors during the season. He wears round prison issue glasses that make him look slightly bookwormish, which is partly due to the fact that he is a voracious reader. While in prison he's become a fan of William Faulkner and Cormac McCarthy, and is currently obsessed with George R.R. Martin's *A Song of Ice and Fire* book series. He knows about the HBO show based on the books, but prisoners don't have access to cable or DVDs and Blu-Rays.

His sense of humor, which was such a part of his personality in high school and one of the things I remembered about him prior to the murder, is still there, but it's not as overt. It's buried more deeply now, and only seemed to come out later in our interview, when Beau was more comfortable.

The last time I remember seeing Beau was in Zimmermann's T.V. production class. We were all a little jealous of Beau; how easily he slipped into the role of morning news anchor, and how funny he was in some of the skits he was in. In another SNL rip-off, Beau starred in a fake commercial that parodied the Zamfir, Master of the Pan Flute commercials that would show up on late-night television. But in Beau's version, his Zamfir is an ex-marine named Willard Gilley, whose dulcet pan flute songs have funny-at-the-time titles like "Die pinko, die!", "Go home, Yankee, go home!" and "What are you, foreign?"

In spite of his popularity, Beau now admits he was "an angry kid" who suffered from low self-esteem and sometimes violent thoughts. While reminiscing about people we used to know, he recalled a friend of mine who used to dress like Robert Smith of The Cure.

"You know, I almost swung on that kid one time," Beau recalled. "One time I saw him wearing an American Flag around his neck. I almost punched him out of the blue...I was always trying to look for something to defend."

Zimmermann was also reminded of times where Beau could be intimidating towards another student. He recalled an altercation during class where Beau and a student who sat in front of him were arguing about something.

"There was some kind of conversation taking place, and at one point I heard Beau say to the other student, 'turn around or I'll kill ya.' It was really chilling the way he said it," Zimmermann said. "At the time I didn't think he was serious, so I told the other student that Beau was just joking and that's just the way Beau was. He was very deadpan. However, after the news came out, I never forgot it, and I know that the other student never forgot it. It was that chilling."

However, according to Johnnie Sue Staples, even in hindsight, there was nothing in Beau's childhood, or adolescence that alerted her or her ex-husband to any of these problems.

On his 17th birthday, Beau enlisted in the Marines, and with his leave date six months away, he was starting to get anxious. He began to feel that he wasn't physically or mentally prepared for the rigors of boot camp and the life of a United States Marine.

"I was terrified of failing, especially after everyone identified me as the guy who was going to go into the Marines," he said. "Being a Marine had become my identity."

To Beau, the idea of what a Marine was came mostly from the movies he watched and the war games he played with his friends. According to both Beau and his mother, from a very young age, he became enamored with all types of war movies, especially *The Green Berets*.

"He was fascinated with watching war movies, he loved *The Green Berets*," Johnnie Sue says. "I don't know how many times he watched that. He had a picture of George C. Scott and John Wayne in his room, so I knew those were people that he admired. In my own personal opinion, TV and movies have a greater influence on children that we can ever imagine."

Beau never felt comfortable speaking to his family about his fears. He tried talking to Mary about the anxiety he was feeling, but she wasn't responsive and Beau admits that at the time he wasn't very good at expressing his feelings.

Beau and his two brothers rarely speak, and his father, who is now divorced from Johnnie Sue Staples, stopped coming to visit and has not called his son in years.

"I was surprised when [Howard Staples] stopped contacting Beau several years ago," Johnnie Sue says. "We divorced after all this happened. Not because of what happened, but we had personal problems and the events put everything in perspective for me—what my priorities are and how I was going to move forward."

As a juvenile being incarcerated along with adult career criminals, Johnnie Sue Staples feared for her son's safety, and not only from the prison population. Early on in his incarceration, Beau and his mother had an agreement that they would keep in touch every two weeks.

"We had an agreement that if he didn't call in two weeks there was something wrong and I had to check into it, and I had to do that once or twice," she says. "I knew that if he didn't call there was something wrong."

In one incident Johnnie Sue remembers Beau being put in solitary confinement because he wouldn't tell officials how drugs were coming into the law library where he was working.

"They did drug tests on those who were working in the library and Beau, of course, wasn't doing drugs, but they wanted him to tell on the others. Squeal, or whatever kind of mobster language you want to call it. He wouldn't do it, so they isolated him because he knew there would be retribution if he told."

Like any mother, Johnnie Sue still worries about her son. She worries about whether he's eating nutritious food while in jail and makes sure to send him money so he can afford to eat at the prison canteen instead of relying on the food served to the prisoners.

"They serve them cabbage," she said. "That's the only vegetable they have. They serve them the cheapest things they can. To me…they should at least let them have gardens so they could have fresh vegetables. What a waste. Why don't they see that that would be great for rehabilitation? It could be something they could learn to do that would be healthy, but they don't have them doing any of that. They warehouse them."

She is also concerned that if he does get released from prison, he will have a hard time getting hired anywhere and he will have not collected any money for retirement. Jonnie Sue became a successful businesswoman after her divorce from Howard Staples. She made enough to support herself, and to put money away for Beau's future. She retired in 2009 after working for the Marriott Corporation for 14 years as a regional director of sales and marketing in their senior living division. She still lives in Florida, although not in the Clearwater/Oldsmar area. She's finished paying for a house she owns in Alabama which she plans on giving Beau when, and if, he is released from prison.

"If he ever gets out he won't have social security because he hasn't worked," she said. "He's trying very hard to keep up with the times by learning computers, but if he gets out I worry that nobody will hire him, probably. That's why I moved to a rural area. My other son has a lot of friends here and a lot of connections, and would likely be able to get him something. I bought the house [in Alabama] so it wouldn't be in a place that would be expensive. All the things I've done have been to try to prepare for him eventually getting out. I worked all the time. I was trying to earn money for myself, but also to think about Beau's future."

In 2007, while in prison, Beau married a woman he knew in middle school, Melissa (Harper) Staples. Melissa says she never forgot Beau because he was always kind to her during middle school.

"I was very shy and I was made fun of a lot and Beau always stood up for me," she said in a recent phone interview. "I never forgot that, even when I heard what had happened."

During his incarceration, they started a letter-writing relationship and it moved forward from there. Although they speak to each other almost daily, Beau says that he tries to write her every Sunday night. "It's the least I can do," he says.

In her letter to the parole board, Melissa writes that Beau is "a respected role model, leader and example for other inmates."

"He has never made excuses for himself, and has always expressed remorse and taken full responsibility for the actions that led to his incarceration," she writes. She also writes that she believes Beau could become a contributing member of the community, and be a responsible husband and father.

Jonnie Sue said she is glad that her son has someone his own age to relate to, especially since the rest of the family no longer keeps in touch with him. She is friendly with Melissa. They talk on the phone occasionally and message each other on the computer. They send each other birthday cards. They've met on more than a few occasions and Jonnie Sue has come to see Melissa as a positive influence on her son's life.

"She seems very nice and pleasant and I think it's helped [Beau] to have her," she said. "He's been in so long, and he doesn't have anyone visit him very often."

Thinking back to his adolescence, Beau admits he didn't know how to express what he was feeling.

"I don't think I ever had good family relationships growing up," Beau said. "My father worked a lot and I didn't see much of him. My brothers were already out of the house."

Even though he was anxious about going into the Marines, Beau said problems and anxieties had been cropping up much earlier. In his sophomore year, he began to associate with an older crowd outside of school. It was at this time he first met Billy at the Burger King where they both worked after-school jobs.

"I always felt like I didn't deserve the popularity I had at school. I didn't feel as smart or deserving of the compliments people gave me at school," he says.

School was like going to a job where he acted one way, and once he was out of school, he felt like he was off duty and free to be a different, less responsible teen.

"I wish I would have hung out with the same people outside of school that I did inside of school, and I got away from that," Beau said. "I was hoping that [going into the military] would give me a purpose and a noble cause. I wanted the self-esteem, and I didn't think I had that at all."

Beau says that it was this low self-esteem that led him to other people with low self-esteem, and to become so incensed by the idea that Billy and Mary had been lying to him behind his back.

Beau agrees with his mother that he watched the movie *The Green Berets* "probably hundreds of times" on videotape by the time he was 14, and would often fall asleep watching it. He said it was through watching movies that he thought he knew what being a Marine was like.

"The whole military thing I was into was twisted from what military life was like," Beau said. To Beau, this twisted sense of the military represented power—power that he wanted to use against the people whom he perceived as wronging him.

"I wanted to show that I was a big guy. I wanted people to see me as somebody you couldn't treat however you wanted to," he says. "I wanted to put my foot down and say 'I'm a badass. I'm a tough guy and you can't get away with doing that to me.' That's what I wanted. I wanted the fear and respect from people. It wasn't even that I hated [Billy] that much. It's so tough to look back at this as a 41-year-old man and put myself in a 17-year-old's position and not think 'what the hell were you doing?' I've tried to rationalize it, and figure out why I did it, but there's no reason. There's just no good reason."

Although he was convicted as an adult, Beau was a juvenile at the time of the murder, and received a life sentence with mandatory 25 years before he was he would be eligible for parole. The sentence was set by mandatory guidelines, leaving Judge Claire Luten no other sentencing option for Beau.

Thirteen months after his arrest, at the request of his council, Beau was interviewed by Dr. Kathleen M. Heide, Ph.D to evaluate his state of mind. After her four-hour interview with Beau, she found him to be sane at the time of Billy's murder, and competent to stand trial. Dr. Heide would go on to interview Beau two more times. After the second interview she used Beau's story (with altered names) as a case study in her book *Young Killers: The Challenge of Juvenile Homicide*.

Dr. Heide's first evaluation included a complete social history of Beau and assessed his level of personal development and the motivations that led him to commit murder.

She reports that Beau was fairly relaxed during the interview and made good eye contact, but that he did experience notable discomfort when asked about the murder. She also writes that Beau didn't refuse to answer any of the hundreds of questions asked of him and that he seemed polite.

"[He] did not appear to be at all manipulative during the interview," she writes. "His responses to questions and his behavior strongly suggested that he was trying very hard to be truthful. His answers to many of the questions, particularly those surrounding the homicide, were anything but self-serving."

However, her evaluation does show that Beau's personality development at the time of his arrest was more characteristic of a younger child than a 17-year-old. According to the Level of Maturity Theory, people progress from level 1 to higher as they resolve problems encountered at each level. Very few people ever attain the ideal social maturity associated with the highest level, level 7. Juveniles who commit crimes usually range from level 2 to level 5. Dr. Heide found Beau to have a maturity level of 3.

"Beau saw the world in black and white dimensions," Dr. Heide writes. "His perceptions of others were deficient...he saw everyone in a particular group as being the same...Beau was relatively incapable of thinking in terms of needs, feelings, and motives in himself and others...his awareness of his feeling states and his ability to discuss them in depth was very limited. Beau was not introspective and was not capable of empathizing with others."

Dr. Heide concluded at the end of her first meeting with Beau Staples that his reflections about his role in Billy's murder were consistent with a low level of maturity.

"He did not experience remorse for killing Billy because he felt that he had been wronged and that he did not have other choices with respect to handling the situation…although he regretted the painful consequences that had befallen him, he was satisfied with the way he was and did not see any need for change."

Five years later, on her second meeting with Beau, Dr. Heide spoke with him for three hours and evaluated his maturity level at a 4 and said that his thoughts about his involvement in the murder had changed significantly.

"Consistent with higher maturity individuals, he saw himself as the person responsible for his behavior and realized that he had choices and did not have to kill Billy," she wrote. "He was able to 'see more of the big picture' and realized how his behavior 'affected a lot of people,' including Billy's family and his own. He felt very badly for the pain he had caused his parents."

According to the 2011 Supreme Court of the United States ruling in the case of Miller v. Alabama, judges are no longer bound by mandatory sentencing guidelines when dealing with juveniles, regardless of whether they were charged as adults for their crime. The decision doesn't invalidate life without parole for juveniles; it applies only when it's mandatory.

The 5-4 decision pitted liberal justices against conservative judges, with the liberal justices writing the deciding opinion, stating, in part, that life sentences for juveniles was unfair due to their moral immaturity and their underdeveloped decision-making abilities in times of stress. Furthermore, the deciding justices stated that mandatory life sentences for juveniles constituted cruel and unusual punishment since they would be serving much longer sentences than those who committed crimes as adults.

While Beau received a life sentence for Billy's murder, his sentencing does not really completely fall under the Miller decision because Beau was offered a chance for parole after 25-years, while some sentences do not. In addition, the cases used to make the Miller ruling are very different from Beau's. In one case, a 15-year-old was the getaway driver during a hold-up. The teen walked into the gas station wondering what was taking so long when the attendant was shot, making the teen an accessory to the murder.

Human Rights Watch, an international non-governmental organization that conducts research and advocacy on human rights, wrote an amicus brief to the U.S. Supreme Court in the Miller decision supporting the ruling. The Human Rights Watch brief quotes brain science studies showing that the human brain doesn't reach full maturity until at least the age of 24. It's a lesson that car insurance companies have learned and it is the reason why insurance rates for young adults don't start going down until the age of 24.

"The body of research that's out there that has been the basis for some of our recommendations is very clear that the adolescent brain is less capable of making rational decisions than that of the adult brain, particularly under stress," says Jobi Cates, Senior Director of the Midwest region of Human Rights Watch. "We're not saying that young people are incapable of making good choices, but what we are saying is...the kind of chemical surge that goes on when they're in a pressure situation...makes them far less capable of understanding the consequences of their actions."

Based on the Miller decision, it's possible that Beau and his attorney could get a judge to reexamine his sentence. However, the Miller decision is not a panacea for Beau. There are other circumstances making Beau's chances of getting his sentencing looked at under Miller slim. Shooting Billy Casey twice in the back, in cold blood, wasn't the only crime Beau Staples is guilty of. There is another charge on his record that further sets him apart from the Miller decision, and could affect his chance for parole.

Chapter 8: A Hit (Part 1)

After being in jail for a little more than two weeks, police intercepted five letters written by Beau to people who either had contacted him, or he wanted to get in touch with.

"God, I hate it in here," he wrote to his first girlfriend Lynette Musante. "In jail time stands still. There are no clocks and where I'm 'being stored' there is no sunlight or chance to go outside. I would have written sooner but before, I wasn't allowed to have a pen or pencil."

In the letter he told Lynette that he had intended on calling her the night "this whole thing happened" just to talk.

"I guess it's a little late now," he wrote. "I'm in isolation because they seem to think I'm dangerous and suicidal. I'm not dangerous anymore and I'm definitely <u>not</u> suicidal. Besides, I want to see how this whole thing comes out, and I couldn't do that if I were dead."

Later in the letter, Beau told Lynette that the state is pushing for the death penalty, but he doubts that they will get it.

"I can't wait to get out of here, but I know it will be a very long time…There is a 25-year minimum sentence for my charge. Jesus, I've only been alive for 17 years," he wrote.

He also tells Lynette that in order to protect himself he couldn't answer the "whys, wheres and whos" until after his trial, but he would like to be able to explain himself to her. He writes that he keeps busy by doing push-ups and an equal number of sit-ups.

"When I finally do get out I will be a lean, mean, lovin' machine (I've had my share of fighting)."

He ends the letter asking her to tell everyone he said hello and to write him.

"Mail helps me forget how bad this place is," he wrote. "Please, don't forget me."

He signs the letter with: I love you and in the PS he asks for a picture, telling her he hasn't seen a pretty face in two weeks.

In another letter, this one to his teacher Mr. Zimmermann, Beau wrote:

"I'm in isolation at the psychiatric ward so they can watch me. They watch me all the time and it's starting to annoy me," he wrote.

He also tells Zimmermann that he can't talk about the specifics of his case, but he does tell Zimmermann how upset he is over some of the statements people at the school have been making about him to the press.

"Who the hell are Katie Marcinkowski and Jeff Truxton! From what I read in the paper they seemed to know me pretty well even though I've never met them," he writes.

He also had a lot to say about his co-anchor, Nancee Madonna, who was quoted in the paper as saying that Beau was a role model in the school and "it's almost a betrayal."

"Where does Nancee get off saying I betrayed her," Beau wrote. "I never liked her and now I hate her with a passion. She had no right to say that."

Beau shares with Zimmermann a lot of the same thoughts about jail life that he did with Lynette, but he also offers this:

"As of now they have no murder weapon and no motive. Sooner or later the motive will come out but no one [will] ever actually know why, except for me."

Beau was questioned about this on the stand at Josh's trial. He admitted to Josh's defense attorney

John Fernandez that he was lying to Zimmermann when he implied there were other motives. Billy's father, who later gained access to these letters, took it to mean that Beau had other motives for wanting Billy dead.

After much debate with her daughter and the rest of her family, Sherry Casey decided against being interviewed for this story. However, she did say that her husband went to his grave believing there was more to the story than Beau's jealous rage. The Caseys believe that Beau also wanted Billy dead because he had been involved in some of the burglaries Billy was locked up for, and that knowledge would have hurt Beau's chances of becoming a Marine. William Casey Sr. died in 2001, and was buried next to his son. Mr. Casey's relationship with his son was always strained and it was hard on him that the two of them never had a chance to reconcile, says his widow Sherry Casey.

Scott Calcaterra says that he became close with the Caseys after Billy's murder, and even sat with William Casey Sr. during Josh's trial. He, too, thinks that some of the motive for the killing had to do with Billy's knowledge of Beau's past crimes.

"Yeah, I do believe that because the reason Billy was in juvenile detention was because he took the rap for all that," Scott says. "Nobody else involved ended up getting arrested and going to juvenile detention. He was the only one. He kept his mouth shut. [Beau] was with him during all of that. I think it was a combination of things, but the bottom line was because of [Mary]."

Beau denies he killed Billy because of any crimes they committed together.

"I never burglarized anything in my life," he says. "Billy didn't know anything that could've hurt me. People want to believe that there is an easy explanation, or maybe something that can help them understand it better, but that's not always the case…It's no more complicated than that…nobody wants to hear that their son's murder was just a recreational activity for someone else. What a horrible thought for a parent's mind to wrap around."

Beau also wrote to a girl from high school named Eva Levicchi, who wrote him looking for answers. Beau doesn't remember what the letter said, or who Eva was, but according to Beau's response at the time, her letter to him must have been sympathetic. In his letter he responded to some of the rumors that were spreading throughout Countryside High School about the killing.

"1) This was NOT a satanic killing! 2) Billy was NOT killed for drugs 3) He was NOT tortured! 4) He was my dearest friend. 5) I am NOT a cold blooded skinhead killer!" He wrote. "Please tell people at school that I told you these things, but don't tell the press… Do not believe the newspapers and television! They just want a good story of a nice kid turned psychotic."

Another important letter Beau wrote from jail was written to Mary Zigmond. It's in this letter that Beau tells her that she knows why this happened and that he wishes her and Billy never met.

"It would have made me much happier and him much more alive if you two had never met, (You know Billy just doesn't have the kick he used to.) I accept all the blame," he wrote.

He tells Mary that she was the first girl he ever truly loved and that he knows that he will be in jail for a very long time. He also tells her to show the letter to no one.

When Beau wrote the letters he was being housed in the medical wing of the county jail.

"It was freezing, brightly lit 24 hours a day and stank of bleach and disinfectant," Beau recalls. "I was severely depressed and thinking about suicide. I was 17 and it was mentally brutal being there with people talking to themselves constantly, or laughing hysterically."

Beau likened it to the wing in which Hannibal Lecter was housed in the movie *Silence of the Lambs*. He said the jail officials made sure he had a pen and paper, envelopes and stamps.

"I was never told my mail could be read. I don't think they had to," Beau admits. "I don't know what I was thinking. I was extremely naïve."

Neither Mary nor any of the other people Beau wrote to would ever see these letters. They were intercepted by jail officials and sent to the FBI for fingerprint analysis to make sure they were written by Beau Staples so they could be used against him if his case ever went to trial.

Beau would never go to trial because there was one more bombshell that was waiting to go off. After being locked up in jail for a little over a year, Beau Staples was caught trying to hire someone to murder the state's witness, Dan Yockey.

Chapter 9: An Accomplice

Surprisingly little is written about Josh Walther in the police report on the murder of Billy Casey and the attempted murder of Dan Yockey. Early on, investigators interviewed fellow students at East Lake High School, but few had much to say about Josh except that he was a big kid, with one girl describing him as a big teddy bear. However, a few people questioned by police recalled Josh making violent statements.

James Sheer knew Josh from a photography class they took together. James told police that he and Josh were talking about war a month prior to the murder.

"Josh made a statement that it would be neat to go to war and kill someone," James said. Josh never made mention that he was planning a murder with Beau.

Christina Lollis also had a conversation with Josh along the same lines. Although she had never met Beau before, she had dated Billy for a few weeks and considered him a good friend. She also knew Josh, and the two spoke over the phone frequently, three weeks prior to Billy's murder.

Allegedly, Josh, out of the blue, told Christina that he wanted to know what it was like to kill someone without having to go to jail. She said Josh told her he didn't want to go to jail because he feared there would be too many homosexuals there.

"I told him he didn't want to know what it was like to kill someone," Christina told police. "I told him: 'That's stupid.'"

Josh allegedly responded that it was true that he wanted to know what it was like to kill someone.

Jennifer Fitts said Josh was allegedly "[running] his mouth off" in art class a few weeks before the murder saying that he wanted to kill someone, and that he wanted to go to a KKK Slaughterhouse meeting where supposedly bodies were hung up on the walls.

Scott Calcaterra knew Josh from school as one of the few students who also liked punk rock.

"I was really weirded out when I found out Josh was involved in this," Scott says. "He was a tall and lanky kid and awkward. Back then I tried to be scary and mean-looking and I know some people thought Josh was intimidating, but I always thought of him as a punk kid into punk rock stuff. I never saw him as someone who was a threat."

Scott says he was in shock that Josh would have gone along with such a plan because, although Josh knew a lot of people in the skinhead group, he was never really a part of the group.

"I think he saw this as a way to prove himself to people," Scott said.

Weeks after Billy's murder, Josh was released from the juvenile detention center on a $25,000 bond and allowed to await trial on the attempted murder charge out-of-state with his aunt and uncle, Joseph and Rose Newcomb in Jonesboro, Illinois.

His mother appeared at that hearing, along with his uncle, Ed Walther, a detective at the nearby Clearwater Police Department. In Jonesboro, Josh registered in a new high school and had a part-time job at a Taco Bell.

Beau avoided serving consecutive sentences and the possibility of being sent to the electric chair by pleading guilty to both the solicitation charge and the first degree murder charge, and he agreed to become the state's key witness in the trial against Josh.

Because of Beau's testimony, which included that he and Josh had planned on killing Billy, Josh was now charged with the first degree murder of Billy and the attempted murder of Dan. With these= new charges against him, the state began the process of extraditing Josh from Illinois and building its case against him.

However, once he was charged, he was again allowed to return to Illinois to await trial, after posting $25,000 bail and agreeing to return for the trial.

According to reports in the St. Petersburg Times, Billy's father, William Casey was furious at the judge's decision.

"I've never seen anyone charged with first-degree murder get off on less than $250,000 bond," William Casey Sr. said. "They both should fry. They've sentenced me and my wife to a life of pain."

Chapter 10: A Hit (Part 2)

Beau is uncomfortable talking about hiring someone to murder Dan. It's a subject he's avoided many times in our correspondence, in spite of me pressing the issue with him, and it's something that he seemed to downplay in our interview. There are differing accounts of how the solicitation took place and all accounts seem to lack pertinent details.

According to the press reports, talk of getting rid of Dan began circulating in the jail in early May of 1990 and detectives learned about the chatter through a confidential informant. By the middle of the month a detective posing as a hit man from Miami met with Beau in the first of several meetings that went on for a few weeks. Beau and the informant never discussed how Dan was to have been killed, but the price for the murder kept being negotiated down. The price for the hit went from $15,000, to $5,000 upfront and $10,000 later, to eventually an agreement of $2,000, which Beau said he would pay once he was out of jail, with money he would raise from "friends in the crack business in St. Petersburg."

The solicitation is mentioned in Det. Desmarais' notes as a single log entry dated May 25, 1990. It says that he received a call from a detective at the

St. Petersburg Police Department, who told him that a confidential source who knows Beau said he was planning to have Dan killed. Desmarais then writes that he opened up a new case file of Beau with the charge of solicitation to commit murder. That file, even 25 years later, remains sealed due to the fact that it contains the names of many undercover informants who could have been used in many other cases. The only other item in Desmarais' notes for this entry is that $500 was requested from a victim's compensation fund to go towards airline tickets to get Dan out of town.

What may be in that sealed file is hinted at in Josh Walther's trial transcripts. At the start of the trial, during the motions *in limine*—where each party makes motions requesting that the judge rule what evidence can and cannot be introduced in trial—Fernandez argued that he wanted to bring up details of the solicitation charge. The state's assistant attorney, David Lichter, disagreed.

"I would be willing to argue…that Mr. Fernandez would be able to state…that Beau Staples pled to the solicitation for the murder wherein he was trying to kill Dan Yockey. I think that's it. I think that's all that's relevant," he said to Judge Luten. "There's a lot more in the solicitation than that…I think it's relevant that they hear that he tried to kill

Dan Yockey. I really do. But I think that's where it stops."

Judge Luten agreed with the state, but Frenandez asked for more clarification as to what he was allowed to say. It would be the first of many times that Fernandez either passive aggressively, or outright aggressively questioned one of Luten's decisions.

"I'm not sure what it is you're granting me. I mean, I need to know the parameters, Judge, as to how far I can go into it," he asked.

"That's how far you can go into it…you can ask him, but not the underlying fact of what he did and who he called and who he contacted…but there isn't any other relevance that I see at this point." she said.

"Your honor," Fernandez tried to counter. "It was a particularly brutal—."

"Mr. Fernandez, that's my ruling, sir," Luten cut him off before he could finish his sentence.

After the murder, and before Dan was flown out of town, Scott and his friends protected Dan, and were very careful about who got near him.

"Dan was a sweet kid," Scott says. "He was just nice easy going kid, and that kid was scared for his fucking life, like nobody's business."

When I was first granted permission to interview Beau at the Avon Park Correctional Institution, I was told I would have no more than an hour to talk to him. I was also told that there would likely be a Plexiglas partition separating us and a guard in the room at all times. Before I passed through the double locked gates, I was given something that looked like an ancient beeper, like the ones doctors used to wear in the '70s. I asked what it was and they told me it was a panic button.

"You shouldn't have a problem with Beau because he's very courteous," the guard told me. "But if anyone gives you any trouble, or says anything that makes you uncomfortable, press the button and guards will swarm the room,"

I suspected that they might have been teasing me. Nevertheless, I clipped the device to my pocket, made sure it was within reach and proceeded into the prison. As it turns out, Beau and I were allowed to sit alone in an unused office in the administration building for three and a half hours. Beau was sitting right across a desk from me with no Plexiglas between us, and no guards watching over.

Since I thought we'd only have an hour, I had prepared a list of questions that I had to make sure Beau would answer directly. As a reporter, you're trained to hold some of the more sensitive questions until the end. One of my last questions was about the solicitation.

In letters Beau delayed telling me about the solicitation two or three times. One time telling me he'd tell me about it later, another time telling me that it was nothing like what was reported in the paper, and then, after a few letters he told me a little more, promising to tell me the rest later.

According to Beau, the solicitation charge was orchestrated by a confidential informant named James "Jimmy" Rubey and the prosecutor's office. (The testimony of James Rubey is listed in court documents, but they were sealed and unavailable.) Beau describes Rubey as "around 40" and says that he later found out, in prison, that he had a history of setting people up who were awaiting trial for big crimes.

"He was a pro," Beau wrote. "He was placed in my pod in the jail and he became buddies with me," He said.

The next time Beau spoke of the solicitation was face-to-face during our interview.

"I'll tell you what happened," Beau said, and for the first and only time in our interview I felt as though I wasn't being told the whole truth, because, unlike his retelling of other events, Beau was short on details about the murder-for-hire scheme, and seemed embarrassed. "I was conned by a professional con man. He was a pro. He took little bits and pieces and wove it into a story and gave it to the detectives. He had me write down the type of ammunition I used on Billy and he later told detectives that this was the type of ammo I wanted him to get to kill Yockey."

Once Rubey was taken out of the jail, Beau said Rubey continued to call him. One time he called the jail saying that he was Beau's brother and there had been a death in the family. When Beau took the call, it was Rubey telling him that he was going to send a guy who was an ex-Navy Seal who would contact him with details about the killing.

"He said, 'help me out, if you use this guy he'll give me a finder's fee.' There was this whole big tale he made up about how he was going to get something out of introducing me to this guy," Beau said.

Beau says he suspected the ex-Navy Seal was a "put on", but he admits that when the guy asked him what he wanted done, he said: "'I want you to kill Dan Yockey.' That was a mistake. A stupid mistake. That was it. Solicitation to commit murder. He tried to press me on it and I told him I had no money and I couldn't pay him anything…I thought I was just stringing this guy along for James Rubey."

His next encounter was a few days later when a woman came to visit him telling him that someone named Dave had sent her. She showed him photos of Dan, and wanted him to confirm that was him.

"I didn't even know if that was Dan Yockey," Beau said. "I couldn't pick him out. I had never met the guy before [Billy's Murder], but I knew the picture didn't look right because it was a shot of a guy getting ready to lay out in the sun and Dan didn't look like the type of guy who lays out in the sun too much, he was kind of a stoner or burnout. The woman kept asking me if it was Dan and I said I didn't know and I had no idea."

Beau says a third person came to visit him and showed him different pictures.

"Now I was getting tired of it. I said I don't care, do whatever you want. That's when they [re]arrested me and told me I was being charged for solicitation to commit murder," Beau said.

Beau now says that he and his attorney discussed fighting the solicitation charge on the grounds that it was entrapment, but had they done that, the state would have used statements made during the solicitation to prove premeditation on the murder charge. If that defense failed, Beau faced the possibility of having to serve consecutive sentences, and he could have also ended up facing the electric chair.

Beau said he wasn't worried about facing the death penalty because, based on what he'd seen in jail, people accused of far more heinous crimes had managed to escape the electric chair. However, he was worried that he would have time for the solicitation added to the 25 year mandatory murder charge.

After the solicitation charge was added, Beau was again placed on 24-hour suicide watch and placed in an observation cell.

"I was extremely depressed," Beau said. "They take everything except a T-shirt and pants. You're barefoot and it's freezing cold. They don't even give you a mattress or a blanket and you're shivering all night long."

He was eventually moved to a psyche-lockdown cell which he describes as being "a dungeon" surrounded by severe mental patients.

"It was brutal. There was nothing more depressing than being there and I wanted to kill myself. I requested my notebooks because I knew I had razor blades hidden in the upper part of the legal pad. When they gave them to me, they were there and I was going to use them to slit my wrists," he says.

Beau brought the blade up to his thumb to make sure the blade was still sharp. He pressed down and ran the blade across, and when he saw his own blood trickle from his thumb, he decided not to kill himself. He still has scars on his thumb to remind him.

To add to the depression, Beau says he knew that he needed to tell his parents about the solicitation charge before the story hit the papers. Unfortunately, he didn't get that chance.

Howard Staples was just returning from his morning walk when he picked up the paper from the box and saw the news, above the fold, that his son was now being accused of trying to hire someone to kill Dan Yockey.

"I got ahold of him the next night," Beau said. "My dad and I were never close so hearing his voice wasn't exactly a comfort… It was another drop in the river of disappointment that my life had become. I hadn't hit rock-bottom, but I was close enough to touch it."

Beau said he doesn't remember when he talked to his mother about the charges, but he knows he did. Talking about the solicitation charge remains an emotional topic for Beau.

Dr. Heide spoke to Beau about the hit five years later, during their second interview. She said Beau's desire to regain power was his reason for participating in the murder-for-hire scheme.

"Beau related that at the time he really didn't care if the supposed hitman killed Dan," she wrote. "Beau recognized he was helpless in jail. If the hitman didn't follow through, Beau felt he was no worse off. If the hitman murdered Dan, however, Beau hoped that it might weaken the State's case against him and send an important message to others."

It was the same kind of message that Beau earlier said he wanted to send to people by killing Billy.

"[The hit] seemed like a quick solution to the problem," Dr. Heide quotes Beau as saying. "I would come out smelling like a rose and looking like I was the one in control."

After her second evaluation of Beau, Dr. Heide concludes that he clearly sees this behavior as being morally wrong.

By admitting to both charges, prosecutors agreed to let Beau serve the solicitation charge at the same time as his murder charge, and not seek the electric chair. He would also get immunity for any other crimes arising out of the murder of Billy, in exchange for a compelling testimony against Josh Walther.

Chapter 11: A Trial

Almost twenty-five years later, Judge Luten, now retired, admits that the trial of Josh Walther and her dealings with Beau were not events that stick out in her career very much.

"There were not very many events that took place in the courtroom," she said. "The solicitation happened so quickly, and at that point in time his fate was sealed. The possibility of him making an entrapment defense fly would have been very difficult. Beau didn't have a heck of a lot of choices left to him."

With Beau's confession to both charges, Luten says Josh's trial was pretty much a clear-cut case of whether Josh helped Beau plan the murder of Billy and whether he intended to kill Dan when he choked him.

The trial lasted five days, and the jury deliberated for less than a day. The jury found Josh guilty of second degree murder on both charges, meaning that they believed he was unaware of any plan to kill Billy and that he did not intend on killing Dan.

If Beau feared Dan was going to be a threat to him if his case had gone to trial, he wouldn't have been too concerned had he seen Dan on the stand at

Josh's trial. Throughout, Dan either didn't remember events that happened, and were in his sworn testimony to the prosecutors, or didn't understand the questions being asked of him. Oftentimes he was contradictory or unclear, and many times he had to be reminded to speak up. The defense had an easy time showing the jury that Dan's memory wasn't the best.

On the stand, Josh seemed very shy and nervous in his grey suit, and sounded more like a scared 19-year-old than a cold-blooded killer, or someone who would try to strangle someone. He said that he had been living out-of-state since the murder because he was afraid of the people Beau knew that may want to harm him. His explanation for lying to Billy about the marijuana was that he thought he was bringing Billy to the woods so that Beau could beat him up. Bringing him to the woods would assure them that none of Billy's friends would get in the way. Josh testified that Beau never said that he wanted to kill Billy. However, once he witnessed Billy get shot, Josh said he was scared for his life and worried that Beau was going to shoot him, too.

"I froze," he testified. "I couldn't move. I thought he was going to shoot me. I was very scared."

The next thing Josh said he remembers was Beau calling him over to help him with Dan. In spite of fearing for his life, he went to Beau to help him.

"The gun was pointed at Danny," he said. "I thought Danny was upsetting Beau because he was screaming and I didn't want Beau to get any more shots out at anyone, so I jumped on Danny and held his throat."

Josh said he wasn't trying to hurt Dan by grabbing his throat, he was only trying to smother him in order to quiet him down so Beau wouldn't shoot the both of them, but Dan began thrashing around. Josh denied that he punched or kicked Dan. He said Dan didn't get knocked out until Beau struck him in the head with the butt of the shotgun, which then went off.

Beau denies that he hit Dan in the face, and the medical examiner's examination of Dan shows that there were no injuries present consistent with being hit on the head.

"I never meant for anyone to get hurt at all," Josh testified at his sentencing hearing. "I didn't know what was going on."

Josh said he never knew that Beau was going to kill Billy and when he realized what was happening, he began to fear Beau and what he was capable of.

However, Josh's statements don't fully agree with a lot of what happened that night, and Assistant State Attorney Lichter made sure to bring that up. Both Deputy Frist and Sgt. Romanosky say Beau and Josh related the made-up story about being shot at in the woods and chased by a van. Romanosky even spoke to Josh apart from Beau to make sure that both of them were telling the same story, giving Josh ample time to tell Romanosky what really happened.

"When the police got there they were in uniforms, guns, everything like that, marked police car that whole deal, right?" Lichter asked Josh. "Of course, being as horrified as you were, you told them exactly what happened out in the woods that night, right?"

Josh didn't get to answer that question due to Fernandez's objection that the questions were argumentative and sarcastic, but, Josh did admit that he lied to police.

Also, Jeff Faust testified that when both Beau and Josh came to his house to try to return the shotgun,

Beau told Josh to get the shotgun from the trunk, which Josh willingly did.

According to both Beau's testimony and Josh's, Beau was throwing up as Josh was trying to smother or choke Dan.

"You didn't take the gun from him at that point?" Lichter asked.

"No," Josh admitted.

During their escape from the woods, Beau gave Josh the shotgun to put in the trunk of the car "because Josh was a faster runner." Both Josh and Beau testified that it was Josh who threw the shotgun off the Courtney Campbell Causeway.

Lichter pointed out that Josh was bigger and stronger than Beau, and yet, despite having the gun in his possession several times, he never tried to escape, in spite of supposedly fearing for his life.

"There is no doubt in my mind that Josh knew exactly what was happening that night," Beau says now. "We bought the ammunition together and had been talking explicitly about murder. No doubt whatsoever."

Josh testified that he did not accompany Beau to buy the ammunition and had no idea the shotgun was loaded.

Scott Calcaterra and William Casey Sr. were also not convinced by Josh's testimony and they let Josh know it from the spectators' gallery.

"Me and Mr. Casey were both asked to stop staring or we were going to have to leave the courtroom," Scott said. "We weren't saying anything, but if looks could kill, [Josh and Beau] would both be dead."

Beau looked at Josh only once in the courtroom, as he was walking up to the witness stand.

"He was staring at the table in front of him. I was so ashamed. I felt like a rat. Even though I should have been pleased to help the Casey family, I felt some loyalty to Josh, still. I felt trapped under an avalanche of complex emotions that I was too young to deal with emotionally, I was suffocating," Beau says.

During his testimony Beau seemed embarrassed when asked by Lichter why he decided to kill Billy. Saying that it sounded really stupid now, but he was upset over the breakup and he thought Billy had been encouraging Mary to break up with him.

"Now that I look back on it, it was really nothing," he said.

Beau now admits that when he was on the stand he was very angry and downplayed Josh's role in the murder because of the loyalty he still felt. He was also still embarrassed by what he had done.

"I felt like an idiot relating what really happened," he now says. "But my pride refused to let me admit that I might have been manipulated into committing a murder. I'm not trying to shed the blame of what I did, but it would not have ever happened if not for the constant encouragement of Josh…I wouldn't have done it by myself. I wouldn't have expended that much effort to find Billy. I was happy just to never see him again and let it all blow over…Josh helped plan it, organize it, and did everything but pull the trigger and serve this life sentence."

Beau has no kind words for Josh, who he refers to as "psychotic" and "abnormally strong, clever and evil." He says that when he thinks back to the night of the murder, he remembers that Josh seemed to be "having the time of his life" and having "fun." He is sure that Josh's intention was to strangle Dan to death and not merely quiet him down because he remembers Josh calling out to him for help, and when the shotgun went off the third time Josh believed that Dan was dead until Beau told him that the gun just went off.

"I really felt like I was through because I was tricked and pressured by the state into the solicitation episode," Beau said. "I was depressed and ashamed...I was trying to sound more at fault than I actually was. God only knows why, but I was trying to help Josh."

Fernandez successfully established that Josh had no reason to want Billy dead and to put the seed of doubt in the jury's mind that Beau's testimony was self-serving.

Josh received a 20-year sentence for his role in the crime. On appeal, Judge Luten reduced his sentence to 15 years. He served six years in a minimum security prison and was released in 1998.

"I don't think Josh was an innocent bystander...I think he knew that something was going to go down," Luten now says. "I think that once they did it he was resigned that they'd done it and he wasn't going to get all upset about it. I don't know if I'd say he was afraid for his life. I never felt that fear for his life was the right emotional statement, I didn't buy that he was coerced into doing anything because of fear for his life."

Luten also doesn't buy Beau's current story about being influenced by Josh to carry out the murder.

"This was not an immature young man," Luten says. "He was an honor student. He made great grades and was in leadership positions in high school. This is a very mature young man. Yes, he was 17, but he knew how to work a crowd and play people… There were a lot of things that I found about Beau that made him very sophisticated for a 17-year-old, and to say that he was led by a fellow like Josh who, quite frankly, did not come off at all sophisticated, is not really believable."

Jonnie Sue Staples offered no comment on Josh Walther, or his sentence, but she does take exception to Judge Luten's comments about Beau's level of maturity.

"Beau was emotionally immature," she said. "Sure he's intelligent and he has a good vocabulary, but not in an emotional problem-solving way. He was sheltered and protected in the way of life in some ways."

In Dr. Heide's case study included in her book *Young Killers: The Challenge of Juvenile Homicide*, she describes Beau (referred to as Jerry Johnson in the book) as being "obsessed with the military." and that it was this obsession, in part, that led Beau to become emotionally stunted in dealing maturely with problems.

"War heroes became his role models," she writes. "He became desensitized to violence. Killing became not only an acceptable solution to problems but also a desirable course of action. He practiced shooting and fantasized killing."

It was his twisted idea of military code that instilled in him the value of loyalty above all else.

My attempts to contact Josh through his aunt and uncle in Illinois were unsuccessful. His aunt, Rose Newcomb, said she would relay the message to him about Beau's current comments.

"Beau is a manipulator and Josh has really worked on getting his life back together and putting this behind him," she said. "He'd rather not comment on any of this."

Chapter 12: A Life

The City of Oldsmar has since redesigned the wooded area surrounding the abandoned sewer facility near National Orange Avenue and Lafayette Boulevard. The entire area which used to be an overgrown soggy marshland is now called the Mobbly Bayou Wilderness Preserve. Where trees and overgrowth once provided cover for a teen hangout, there are now well-lit, wide open fields, exercise apparatus, a dog park, a butterfly garden, picnic tables and boat launches. The old water tank which during the investigation was drained to look for the weapon that killed Billy Casey has been converted to an observation tower. Murals of wildlife replace the graffiti that used to be all over the tank and the other structures that have been left standing. Next to the structures, where Beau Staples shot his friend twice in the back over an argument about a girl, and Josh Walther allegedly tried to strangle Dan Yockey to death, there is a playground where parents are required to supervise their children. There is no mention of Billy Casey Jr. at the site.

Dan Yockey did not wish to contribute to this story. I contacted him though Facebook and left him multiple messages assuring him that I would keep his whereabouts a secret. He never responded and eventually deactivated his Facebook account. As it turned out, Gary Yockey and I share an acquaintance. After contacting Gary, he responded by asking me to leave his family alone, a request which I respected.

Except for a weapons charge that he was later exonerated of, Beau has been a model inmate. While in prison he's learned cabinet making and learned how to fix small engines He's earned certificates in Victim's Awareness and Domestic Violence Against Women. At one point Beau served as a prison law clerk, doing legal research and helping other inmates file legal motions, but he became disillusioned with that when he felt his efforts were futile. He subscribes to a few computer magazines, Vanity Fair, USA Today and The Wall St. Journal. While in jail he became computer literate and does a little database design programing, and he's currently learning web design. However, even though the prison has Internet access for the staff, inmates are restricted from going online.

Beau says his cell is probably a little bigger and nicer than the 8' x 5' cell the warden described.

"We have a table, a sink, some shelves," Beau said describing his cell. "I've been here a while, and I used to work for maintenance so I was able to get some stuff, so my cell is real nice. If you're a lifer you usually can maneuver and get things. I have a big glass mirror instead of a little metal mirror. If you know how to get it, and have the right job, you have access to things. If you're useful, they'll let you slide on comfort things."

Beau said he very rarely gets bored in prison. He keeps busy by reading, his job and with his softball team.

"I've never had any problems filling time," he said. "Me and a couple of other lifers were talking about this. I said I never get bored and they all agreed with me. As a lifer, you manage to always find ways to interest yourself. If there's one thing you can do is time. A guy told me this when I first got locked up, he was a Vietnam vet, he said, 'Kid, the human mind can adapt to anything. You're stronger than this. You can do anything. Just sit down and do whatever you have to do. Don't ever think you can't do this,' and he was right. That stuck with me a long time. You can adapt to the worst conditions imaginable."

I said to Beau that many people will read this and think 'this isn't punishment. He's learned to adapt to this life, and that's not retribution.' Beau says that he thinks about what he did every day and he wishes he could take it back.

"I think about it," Beau said. "Why didn't I just call the cops? I knew where [Billy] was most of the time…that would have taken him out of the picture, but that seemed, and it sounds bizarre now, but that seemed kind of dishonest whereas I chose a murder, but calling the cops on somebody seemed cowardly, and taking someone out into the woods and shooting an unarmed person didn't. I can't explain it to where it makes sense because none of that makes sense."

Approaching middle age has given him a perspective that the teenaged Beau would never been able to foresee.

"I can see the damage and the hurt I've caused, not just to Billy Casey, but his entire family and mine," he wrote recently. "What I hate the most is that I'm depriving my mother of a son she can be proud of and my wife a husband," he said. "I feel that I can deal with anything, but I'm forcing them to take on problems they shouldn't have to. I forced a lot of people to deal with things, both emotionally and financially, they shouldn't have to deal with."

When we spoke, I said to him that many people believe that murderers can't be forgiven and should never be let out of jail. I asked him if he felt 25 years inside prison was enough to pay for what he's done.

"I've thought about this before and talked about it with other guys in here, in my situation," Beau said. "What's enough time? Some guys in here would think 5 years. Nobody thinks they should never get out. Nobody thinks that. It's hard for me to say because I want to say, yeah, I've done enough time. I believe that my personal development and my maturity has gone as far as it needs to go to keep me from committing any crimes or making any choices that would lead to anyone else being hurt. I've done enough time to do that. As far as punishment goes? I believe I have, but I'm sure if you ask the Caseys they'd disagree. And who's right and who's wrong? I don't know. I can't be the decider if I've done enough time, and realistically, they can't either. This is some type of Old Testament type judgment. That's what the parole board is supposed to do."

When we first started talking about his parole hearing, Beau seemed sure that there was no chance he would get out, saying that in his 25 years in prison, he's never seen an inmate serving a life sentence for murder get paroled their first time around.

"It happens, but in all that time you'd think I'd have met one," he said. "I haven't."

As the date for the hearing got closer, Beau sounded more excited about the possibility he would be released.

"It's been said that if a victim's family attends and opposes your parole, then it is always denied," he wrote. "I sincerely hope that there are only friendly faces in attendance. I'm ready to get out."

In preparation for his hearing Dr. Heide conducted a third interview with Beau. This time she met with Beau for five and half hours. She also interviewed his wife, his mother, both brothers and his father. In her report she writes that Beau's chances of reoffending are low. She evaluates his maturity level at a 5 which is a high level of development and not one commonly encountered in offender populations.

"Based on more than 30 years evaluating offenders, I am firmly convinced that Beau is genuinely remorseful for the killing of Billy Casey and for the harm his actions caused Dan Yockey," Dr. Heide writes. "He feels very badly for the pain he has caused his parents, Billy Casey's parents, Dan Yockey and his former girlfriend Mary because he is able to see the situation from their perspectives today, whereas at age 17, he could only see his point of view."

Dr. Heide concludes her evaluation by referring to the same studies Human Rights Watch cited in their brief to the Supreme Court of the United States. Dr. Heide goes further, stating that the last part of the brain to develop in juveniles is the part of the brain that is critical in evaluating information, making judgments and thoughtful decisions, planning and organizing. She describes this part of the brain as the "part of the brain that puts the breaks...on the emotional part of the brain, allowing us to think before we act impulsively."

This emotional maturity is something Beau said he's spoken to Dr. Heide about in length.

"I don't feel like I reached full emotional maturity, where I was truly thinking clearly about what I had done, until about 15 years into my incarceration," he said. "I wasn't truly remorseful until then and who knows, I may not even be there yet. I hope I'll continue to grow. I've used this time to work on myself and change the person I was."

Also included in his parole package, is a single page "Personal Message on Self-Improvements" letter. The letter comes off sounding slightly boilerplate and a little academic. He writes that he is remorseful and has matured while incarcerated, and that he bases his thought processes on empathetic rational decision-making and not personal feelings.

"In conclusion," he writes. "I have completely changed the way I think, therefore changing the way I feel, and thus changing the way I react to situations. The teenager that committed this murder is gone and in his place is a mature 41 year old man, ready to take his place in responsible society to be a living example that the justice system can be both punitive and rehabilitative."

Along with his statement, Beau's wife, mother, brother and a few family friends also wrote letters supporting his parole.

"I think I'm ready because my expectations are realistic," Beau said to me when I asked him if he felt prepared to reenter society. "I don't expect to get out and become a millionaire and everyone will love me and want me over [to] their house for dinner and to hang out. I want to be able to be with my wife, go to work, work hard."

One of the things Beau said he would like to do is help troubled teens who were like him and work with younger prisoners.

"I think I'd be good at speaking with at-risk youths," he said. "I would like to help somebody. I've tried to help people here and I've gotten a lot of satisfaction about that and I think I would help build a lot of self-esteem."

Johnnie Sue says her son is too modest and didn't include in his parole package all of the work he's done with helping young prisoners in jail.

"He's helped them work on their legal appeals, he even helped one of them learn to read," she says. "In fact, I sent him reading workbooks so that Beau could teach him and that boy left prison knowing how to read. He's been a good influence on people in there."

I also asked him if he was prepared for either the possibility of a long wait to be paroled, or never be granted parole.

"Even if I have to stay in prison for the rest of my life, I feel like I could be at peace with that," he said. "I feel like I'm genuinely, terribly sorry for what I did, whether the Caseys accept that or not, I just don't want them to think I'm sitting here all smug about it. I could never make it up to the Caseys and I can't expect them to ever think, 'yeah, Beau should be let out.' I would just hope, for my own selfish reasons, they wouldn't oppose my parole. The murder of one human being affects so many others, I see that now. As a teenager I had no concept that I could do something in [Oldsmar] and make a woman who lives across the country cry 25 years later. That's incomprehensible to a teenager."

Billy's memory lives on with his family, including a half-sister he never really got a chance to know, and in his friend Scott Calcaterra, who has a tattoo of a cross on his arm that reads: In Memory of Billy Casey.

Scott now owns a tattoo parlor and lives in Virginia with his girlfriend and his son. Unlike a lot of people he hung around with at the time of the murder, he's survived and gotten his life in order. It upsets him that Billy never got that chance.

"I never forget his birthday, October 12th. I'll never forget April 10th. Those are two really important days for me," Scott said. "I think [Beau] should rot in jail forever. Honestly. I really think he deserves to spend the rest of his time in jail. I don't care what kind of clown he's become, or what he says and I hope he never sees the outside again. He denied my son of meeting someone who I considered a brother. He denied my son of an uncle, and he robbed me of someone who I believe would have been a life-long friend."

Understandably, Johnnie Sue Staples feels differently about her son. She does not think it is within her son to ever be dangerous again. She says she now sees that at the time, Beau was a very emotionally immature young man who didn't imagine the consequences of his actions.

"I think Beau was very young when he made a bad, bad decision and he's paid for it," she said. "He's remorseful. He would do anything to take it back. He understands now how it has impacted not only his life, but a lot of other people's lives. He's so sorry for it. Having said that, it's not doing anybody any good for him to stay in prison. He could be out and try to be useful in this society and use this experience to try to help others not make a mistake like that. With all the youth violence that's going on now, maybe there's something he can do to help somebody."

Beau's parole hearing took place in June of 2013.

According to Johnnie Sue Staples, the prosecutor for the State of Florida brought up the fact that the day before the murder, Beau attended a skinhead party. The party in question was the one he, Mary and Billy attended. According to Beau's testimony which is corroborated by the police report, the party was not a skinhead party.

"Beau attended the party, and a couple of skinheads showed up, but it wasn't a skinhead party." Johnnie Sue said. "When the guy from the State Attorney office said [it was a skinhead party], you could see the look on the faces of the parole board. It's like they were trying the case all over again. They didn't look at now, or what type of person he's become, they just looked at the crime."

The parole board set a presumptive parole date of April 11, 2029 – 40 years and a day after Billy Casey's murder. Beau will come before the board again in November of 2019, at the age 48. Depending on his behavior in prison, the 2029 release date could be pushed back or forth, or stay the same.

Photos

Beau during our 2013 interview at the Avon Park
Correctional Institution in Avon Park Florida.
PHOTO BY SCOTT WACHTLER

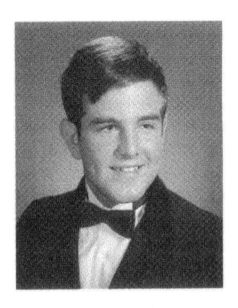

Beau's 1989 Countryside High School Yearbook Photo. PHOTO COURTESY OF THE PINELLAS COUNTY HISTORICAL SOCIETY

Josh Walther's junior year yearbook photo from the 1989 East Lake High School Yearbook. . PHOTO COURTESY OF THE PINELLAS COUNTY HISTORICAL SOCIETY

A playground is now located at the site of Billy Casey's murder. The water tank and the concrete structures remain and have been painted over.

PHOTO BY SCOTT WACHTLER

Acknowledgments

Besides the people who I interviewed for this story, there are a number of family members and friends who deserve thanks for helping me get this off the ground. Top on the list is my editor and wife Ella Shenhav who supported me when I told her I wanted to quit my job as the editor of the *Cambridge Chronicle* in Cambridge Massachusetts three months before our daughter was born so that I could begin work on this. She gave me the time to visit Beau in prison, interview people, track down police reports, medical records and trial transcripts. With her background in law, she helped me translate legalese into understandable English, and she helped me struggle though the story when I had no idea where and how to begin. She also gave me valuable time after our daughter was born, while we were still learning how to be new parents, and still sleep deprived, to go to the Brookline Public Library to bang out the first draft of the story which always seemed to need just one more week, one more day before it was something that looked like a first draft. She (mostly) didn't complain when piles of notebooks and folders filled with police logs and transcripts began to fill our tiny Boston apartment. And it was Ella who encouraged me to keep at the story, even when it looked like I wasn't getting anywhere with it. Put simply. You wouldn't be reading this book if it weren't for my wife, and for that, she deserves the highest thanks.

Thank you to everyone who sat through me telling you the story, sometimes inelegantly, with no form and little substance; it was in these discussions where I feel the story came together. Hearing how people reacted to various twists and turns helped me form the skeleton of the story and create what I hope is a compelling narrative. Thanks also to Tom Cates and Ignacio Laguarda for being the first people (after Ella) to read the first draft all the way through and point out inconsistencies, redundancies and my usual sloppy punctuation.

Thank you to Joe Mont, David Harris and Mark Miller. Two of my former editors and one of my oldest friends, and three of the best journalists and writers I know. They offered some much needed advice on how best to tell this story and they've always showed me what it means to be a great reporter, journalist and a writer.

Thank you to my parents, Bonnie and Mac Wachtler who made me a curious reader and always encouraged me when I told them I wanted to write.

Lastly, (and most certainly not least) thank you to Tony Strauss who besides being one of the kindest, gentlest and most astute copy editors I've ever worked with, is also one hell of an artist, and one hell of a good friend for offering to help me out on this with copy editing and cover design.

I could not have done any of this without the help of all these people and many, many more.

Author's Bio

Scott Wachtler worked as a journalist in the Boston area for over seven years. He's written for the *Bulletin Newspapers*, *BostonNOW*, *The Harvard Law Record*, *The Needham Times* and *The Cambridge Chronicle/TAB* where he was the assistant editor and eventually the editor. He has published short stories in *Gallery Magazine* and in *The Crow's Nest.* Most recently he has worked as a contributor to *Weng's Chop* magazine, a genre cinema mag dedicated to all cinema weird and wild.

When he's not writing, he's a proud stay-at-home dad who loves going on adventures with his daughter, Serena.

34234958R00073

Made in the USA
Charleston, SC
04 October 2014